Dr. Will's Guide To How To Be *(Like)* A Therapist

(Even If You Are Not A Therapist)

Dr. Will Miller

Dr. Will's Guide To How To Be *(Like)* A Therapist
Even If You Are Not A Therapist

Contents[1]

Introduction

Chapter 1: On Being Like A Therapist: Walk The Walk

Chapter 2: On Being Like A Therapist: Talk The Talk

Chapter 3: On Being Like A Therapist: Heal Thyself

Chapter 4: Understanding Symptoms and Treatment

Chapter 5: Honing Your Craft: Clinical Case Studies

Chapter 6: Final Exam

Oath

Certificate of Completion

---

[1] Due to the confidential nature of the material included here, this book has **not been edited**. If you find any text errors such as spelling or grammar, ignore them and move on. And don't be writing me letters about it. Try not to be so anal, Sparky!

CHAPTER OUTLINE

Chapter 1: On Being Like A Therapist: Walk The Walk

Sharing his years of experience as a professional therapist, Dr. Will shows you how to *appear* like a real therapist. He covers the proper facial expressions, emotional reactions, physical distance from others and even creating the proper dress and manner of a shrink.

Chapter 2: On Being Like A Therapist: Talk The Talk

In addition to *appearing* like a real therapist the book delves deeper into the area of *sounding* like a therapist. Here we cover vocal inflections, to speak or not to speak, choice of words, even what terms to use and avoid.

Chapter 3: On Being Like A Therapist: Heal Thyself

The journey continues going ever inward to the complex area of the reader's own psyche. Dr. Will guides you to a new understanding of your own personal nature and making sense of your childhood. He shows you how to use the mess of your own life to relate to the mess of the other person. All just like a real shrink!

Chapter 4: Understanding Symptoms & Treatment

Now that you are ready to pretend you are a therapist, we open the door to the tools of the trade, including the maps and guides real shrinks use to label others. With study you will be able to spout clinical terms and bandy about lingo that will impress anyone in a meeting, at the office or on a hot date.

Chapter 5: Honing Your Craft: Clinical Case Studies

Here is an opportunity to feel like a real therapist as you read actual, fictional case studies and take a crack at diagnosis and treatment options. You will be tested on what you have learned and have the thrill of accomplishment. This is what it is like to be a working shrink!

DEDICATION

This is dedicated to...

Professor Billy Lynbrook who once told me *"you'll never, ever be a shrink."* Well read on Billy & stick it!

And ...

Maggi Ingleman, therapist extraordinaire, who encouraged me to be a therapist. Thank God she didn't live to see this.

And ...

The family at **The Bob & Tom Radio Show**: my patients for 20 years. Bob, Tom, Chick & Kristi have provided a rich laboratory for my analytic skills. They are each and all brilliant, sane, healthy & wise beyond their years. I am a better therapist because of them *(I think)*

Forward

Dr. Will Miller, America's renowned, public pop psychology therapist is considered by some to be one of the country's leading therapeutic experts.[2] For years he has offered his insights to America, cutting his teeth analyzing television characters on *Nick-at-Nite*. He is currently the official Psychotherapist for the cast and audience of the nationally syndicated **Bob & Tom Show**. They report strong spikes in their personal & collective healing.

Now, for the first time, he is making his insights available to you - the ordinary thinker - so you too can wield the power of pop psychology for life improvement, and perhaps even a profitable career. This manual will change your life! And we guarantee that if it fails to make you successful and affluent, you need to re-read and apply the techniques correctly. It is a significant work that includes more than a dozen footnotes.

With this 'easy to read and apply' guide you can:

- Learn psychology the easy way. Learn tricks therapists use to see through people's expressions and understand their motives and intentions

- Disarm friends, family and strangers with your quick insights into their character and motivations

- Increase your powers of perception that will enable you to intervene in critical situations, work with the police and the government and develop amazing bonds with animals

Why wouldn't you do this? Aren't you worth it? Isn't this your time? Dr. Will is allowing you to take this class without paying tuition, just this text fee. Isn't he great? He got all the degrees, so you don't have to!

DISCLAIMER: Dr. Will does not of condone the misuse of therapy for personal gain. This does not mean, however that you cannot profit from the advice offered in this book. We just advise that you do so paying adequate attention to ethics as you understand the term. Further, if you are prissy, thin skinned or a defensive therapist in real life, perhaps you should not proceed *(unless you are willing to get a cold eyed glimpse of how other people actually view us)*

---

[2] No official state or federal organization recognizes Dr. Will as a leading expert in this field.

Introduction

Have you ever been consumed with envy when listening to a therapist on the radio or TV, when they casually describe what is wrong with someone, perhaps you? Do you believe that a trained therapist has the ability to read your mind? Well it's true! Therapists usually can see right through you! Do you wish you could do the same? Well, you can! And without the stress and pressure of years of training and formal education!

Let Dr. Will show you how

This guide is a straight forward look at what makes someone look and act like a therapist in public situations. It will help you turn your common, everyday encounters with strangers into an opportunity for healing. By reading this book and studying the techniques you will be able to legitimately say to people, "I'm studying to be like a therapist."[3] You will soon be walking, talking and even dressing like an actual therapist. And why wouldn't you want to do this for yourself? We all know that people simultaneously revere and fear therapists. Much like your parents and grandparents who know you so well that they see through your phony facade, therapists also make you feel at once comforted and exposed. The difference is that, unlike these close family members, a therapist is trained to avoid provoking guilt and shame. Which means they are gentle with your inner child. Isn't that great? Read on and find out how you can become a person who understands people without infuriating them like their family![4]

Again, let Dr. Will show you how!

---

[3] Be sure to accent the words *'be'* & *'a therapist'*, glossing over the word *'like'*
[4] **NOTE**: Under NO CIRCUMSTANCES are you to offer advice or prescriptions!

Chapter 1: On Being Like A Therapist: Walk The Walk

The chapter title should perhaps read: how to appear to be a therapist whether or not you are one in reality. Because when it comes to functioning like a therapist, appearance becomes the reality. In this chapter we cover the five basics that include:

1. Facial Expressions
2. Emotional Reactions
3. Physical Distance
4. Redefining Personal Relationships
5. Creating the Proper Physical Appearance

Facial Expressions

Guarding Your Face:
The key to the therapeutic expression is what we call "flat affect." This means that your face registers no evident emotion as someone is telling you the most shocking things. Therapists never casually wink, tsk or roll their eyes in front of someone. The clinician always has a laser focus on the other person which serves to at once communicate "I'm listening and attending" as well as intimidating the person into telling you their secrets. Facial control is a critical first skill to master.

Let's practice:
Using your smart phone, record yourself watching episodes of the Jerry Springer Show. Later review yourself and notice your facial expressions. Do you easily react to the surprising or revolting content of the show? This is your baseline. What expressions did you use? Were they appropriate? When a guest began weeping over their emotional pain, did you start weeping as well?[5] Practice this exercise over several weeks until you can maintain a straight face regardless of the content of the show.

Reading Other Faces:

---

[5] If you said laughter, see Chapter 5 on treating your own issues.

Human beings have the gift (some say the curse) of very expressive faces. And part of your job to be like the therapist is being able to read the faces of others. And this involves two variables: first, you must master interpreting the emotion that a particular facial expression is telling you. Second, and this is disturbing, many people, consciously or unconsciously, are able to mask their emotion with a straight face. This is just like the face we've advocated you develop above. This does not mean that they are intending to do it. There are three possibilities: 1. They might have a condition that limits their facial expression; 2. They are deceitful; 3. You are looking to the face of another therapist, in which case the tide is now turned and you are helpless.

Let's practice:
Ask your significant other or a close friend to purposefully exhibit various emotions (happiness, rage, sadness, confusion, etc). Once you are familiar with the range of their facial expressions, abruptly say something hateful to them. for example, *"My God I couldn't believe what they said about you. I would be devastated!"*
Now observe their next facial reaction and name it to them out loud. The statement needs to come as a complete surprise after your prior, friendly conversation. Once you have registered their reaction, assure them that it was not true and they should calm themselves.

Emotional Reactions

The more you learn to behave like a therapist you'll notice that others will begin to behave differently around you. This is because people become anxious when facing a therapist. They suspect that just by observing them we can tell what is going on within them, particularly what is "wrong with them." This is not true, we do not know exactly *what* is going on with them *(what is true, of course, is that we can tell that something is wrong, just not necessarily what)*. Suffice it to say that in the presence of a therapist an individual is always back on their heels.

But returning to the issue at hand ...

Exuding a therapeutic posture means that people will be alert and exhibit a reaction that demands you be prepared. It will go in one of two directions.

Either:
They will drop their defenses and feel inclined to approach you, emotionally and often physically. You will find that such people will begin sharing very personal information with you, even confessing emotionally sensitive and painful stories about their lives. In such cases it is imperative that you react appropriately. What they tell you might surprise and shock you, and here is where your face training is critical. If they sense that you are not ready to hear what they are saying, your expression will show it and their trust in you will shatter like dropped egg. If you do become defensive they will feel rebuffed, become wounded and perhaps even attack you. You need to be ready to defend yourself.

Or:
They will become rigidly defensive and begin to emotionally and physically withdraw from you. This might be subtle, with foot shifting and eye blinking. Their fear of exposure can rouse their most primitive defenses in parts of their brain that ignite a fight or flight response. Again, reacting appropriately is imperative, because your own brain's defense systems will be aroused as well. Your *pretend* therapeutic reaction means remaining neutral, resisting the temptation to either ridicule or persist in questioning them. When it is obvious they are not prepared to share, it is imperative once again, to react appropriately. Change the subject to something benign such as the weather or a local crime story. Resist personal notices such as their attire or hairstyle as these might be misinterpreted and trigger a reaction, even violent. Here too you must be prepared to defend yourself.

Let's practice:
Ask an acquaintance to find a volunteer, someone they know but who does not know you. Tell them you are part of a research project and would like them to participate in an experiment. Tell them it pays the standard rate for clinical trial participation *(between five and 10 dollars for a fifteen minute*

session)[6]. Have them enter a room and sit alone. The session must be video recorded. Have an assistant, clad in a lab coat and holding a clipboard, enter and tell them that a trained therapist will be in shortly to interview them. Before leaving the room have the assistant take the person's pulse.[7] Next you enter the room and introduce yourself. *(DO NOT say you are a therapist as this could open you up to charges of fraud and prosecution)*. Simply ask them how they are doing and then observe their physical reaction. Note whether they drew closer or farther away. Did they begin to perspire or fidget? Their reaction will be your first, early evidence of how your presence affects people who suspect that you are a real therapist. Review the video and repeat the experiment with others until you feel you have mastered the emotional posture of a professional shrink.

Physical Distance

With time and experience you will soon master the crucial variables involved in appearing to be a therapist. You will learn to control your facial expressions at the most subtle level. You will not yield to temptations of showing your emotions with your face. You will even learn to repress inclinations for facial-tics or rapid-eye-blinking that betray your feelings. You will also control your own emotional reactions so as to remain neutral or blank slate to the person you are facing.

Next you will need to learn the proper physical distance to maintain between yourself and the other. This should be obvious that standing too close too far away communicates important information to the other person. But we are not talking about your comfort, but that of the other individual. Standing closer than they like feels intrusive and will shut down communication. Standing too far off suggests that you are turned off by them and want to get away. Even if either of these are true, you must curb your own desires and find the proper space.

---

[6] It is advised that you tell them to report this income to the IRS.
[7] It is not necessary to actually take their pulse. Just hold their wrist and pretend to calculate. IMPORTANT: Be sure the person is looking at an actual watch!

Let's practice:
Using a volunteer, preferably someone you know well. Select a topic that is uncomfortable to speak about, perhaps an issue with their family or a work colleague that will spark agitation in the other person. For example, begin by saying *"you know the big rumor about you in the office has to do with your slovenly appearance ..."* The purpose here is to evoke a clinical situation that rouses emotion and will affect physical comfort.

This exercise is staged in two separate sessions. In the first case, ask the person to wear an appealing cologne that will affect your comfort being close. In the second round have the person hold a small bowl of sauerkraut or other pungent food product that will cause you to stand off. Your job is to focus exclusively on the conversation without paying conscious attention to the sensory distractions. At the end of each round, measure the space between you. The average of the two is the proper clinical distance.

Redefining Personal Relationships

As you slowly and methodically begin to apply the techniques you learn here, it will certainly affect all of your personal relationships. Everyone from your significant other, your kids and family members, as well as co-workers and neighbors will notice the change that has come over you. They might ask, "Have you lost weight?" Some will worry that you are ill or suspect that you are in some crisis. Still others might conclude that you are now insane.

How will you handle their reactions? While some will say it outright *("what the hell is wrong with you")* most will simply avoid the subject and no longer make eye contact with you. But don't panic, you can work through this phase and come out with either stronger connections to them or happily shed your dysfunctional relationship with them once and for all. *Buh-Bye!*

Some have chosen the radical option of simply relocating to another city and state, beginning fresh with new people who come to know the new, therapeutic you. This is a very tempting option. But clearly it's impractical to abandon your current responsibilities for family and work. If it is possible, however, you can begin a new life with all new relationships with the great advantage of appearing like a therapist from the get go! Think about it.

Let's practice:
Here are a few quick tips to minimize the reactions your new behavior will evoke:
- Always carry around a copy of the DSM-V manual.[8] Have it be visible to everyone who sees you. When casually walking around, open it up and *(pretend to)* read any page at random. Nod your head and audibly mutter "huh" as if gaining new insights.
- Always have a notebook in hand and visible. Stop and write notes as you look around at others.
- Get the "Fake A Call" free app for your smartphone and act out a one-way conversation with a "client" you appear to be helping. Pepper your end with phrases like, "No Barry, it's ok. Practice your breathing" and "That's good Louise, I'm proud of you for standing up for yourself. No...there's no need to thank me. It's why I'm here." *(Be sure to include convincing pauses)*.
- Learn to turn a conversation back around by asserting your therapeutic posture with a reply like "it seems you are uncomfortable in our relationship. Do I remind you of someone else in your life? Someone with whom you had conflict? Someone who hurt you?" Even if they react with agitated defensiveness you have altered the entire chemistry of the conversation. You'll be amazed at the change in energy flow

---

[8] The Diagnostic Statistical Manual is the Bible for all mental health professionals. It is hundreds of pages and worth the price. You will find everything wrong with yourself and everyone you know. It's a blast.

Creating the Proper Physical Appearance

If you are walking through the mall and observe the people strolling around, could you tell which one might a therapist? Not likely. However, you could certainly identify those who are probably *NOT* therapists. Even after accounting for children and adolescents, which adults are probably not clinicians? For instance, the man with the face tattoo or the woman with the multi colored hair and nose ring seem unlikely candidates. The middle age man wearing tight fitting short shorts is probably not a shrink. Nor is the lady wearing combat boots and welding goggles. Just saying.

But what about that guy with the tweed jacket and round glasses? The smartly dressed woman in the business pantsuit carrying a leather attaché case? Obviously you are getting warmer. What do we learn from this mental exercise? Therapists are not models out of *Vogue* or *GQ*. But they are not likely individuals who look like complete idiots in public. Again, just saying.

What's the take away here? It boils down to using your head and do what instincts tell you about how to manage your therapeutic appearance. As my first instructor once said to us in class on the topic: "Don't be an ass! If you want to be taken seriously, take your garb seriously!" Let's consider some guidelines:

The Elements of Therapeutic Style

The fundamental guideline here is managing and avoiding visual distractions. So let's begin from the ground up:

Footwear:
Find something between spiked heels and tattered sneakers. Shrinks need to wear comfortable footwear. Remember: the patient is sitting in front of you and if you cross your legs they see your knees and feet. Watch their eyes - they notice your kicks! They will be distracted by what they look at and, importantly what they smell!

Lower Wear:
Pressed slacks or designer jeans. Never wear skirts in seated conversations for obvious reasons. And recalling the legs crossed position above, seeing your boney ankles or fleshy thighs adds nothing to the therapeutic exchange. These are scenes they cannot *un-see!*

Upper Wear:
Neat, professional tops and shirts are necessary. Never permitted are tank tops, tube tops or shirts with obscene logo's. Watch their eyes. Are they looking at your eyes or somewhere else?

Coif & General Appearance:
Do you really need to be told that a Mohawk or flamboyant hats are therapeutic show-stoppers? Even in the South a real therapist is not wearing a cowboy hat in session. No muttonchops, dental grills or facial ink. Neat and trim people!

Fashion Accents:
Consider certain appealing, smart looking additions including: trimmed facial hair (*men only*), round frame eyeglasses, sleeve patches always work. Use Google images and search "therapist" to get more ideas.

SIDEBAR

They Walk Among Us

Just Who Are These Therapists?

Therapist is a generic term describing anyone who treats or heals another. The word comes from the Latin word **therapia** that means, of course, shrink. There are three basic ways to become a real therapist *(not your real concern here as you will be skipping this entire process)*:

Psychiatrist: This is a medical doctor who went through the time and expense of becoming a physician and then made the bizarro choice to specialize in this kooky field. They mostly prescribe drugs and, although there are many exceptions, they tend to be abrupt, impatient and will just spit out what's wrong with you, ready or not. "Oh yeah, you're bipolar out the wazoo!"

Psychologist: These are the professionals who understand your mental state and verify what's up with you using tests and measurements. Big into studies, they train by watching lab animals and then apply their habits to us. Weird as it sounds, it generally works well in diagnosing you, even if you sense they are looking at you as if at a rhesus monkey. These are the shrinks who testify against you in court. "Yes, your honor, in my opinion, he knew exactly what he was doing with the hammer."

Social Worker: The largest crop of shrinks, their training is all over the map ranging from hard core psychoanalysts through new age, past life practitioners. No one can get a handle on what each one actually knows, so trying them out until you have a good vibe is a must. They are typically the most sympathetic, as they understand the feeling of being professionally marginalized and unappreciated. They usually have the most mysterious letters after their name. With careful investigation they can be awesome and are generally the least expensive path to sanity. But they can take you down the rabbit hole in a few sessions if you're not vigilant.

Chapter 2: On Being Like A Therapist: *Talk The Talk*

The clearest way to tell if someone is a therapist is by listening to how they speak. Therapists are highly observant people. In fact they are way more observant than the average civilian. On the perception hierarchy they rank immediately below spiritualists, psychics, shamans and Sherpas. The difference is that therapist's work is done in the gritty reality of life, not in some airie-fairie altered states of consciousness or some high mountain-top. Shrinks are people of the street, not the clouds! They have developed a keen eye for patterns of behavior and word associations that give away the secrets of those around them. And based on these observations they also develop an instinct for what to say and what not to say, at least out loud.

So how can you, with no formal training, imitate this approach to communication? It's not as difficult as you might think. Let's begin with how you sound.

Obviously being like a therapist includes learning to talk like they talk. You can cultivate the look and presentation all day long, but if all you do is stand by mute as others share their human suffering you'll be dismissed as a useless dolt. But here's the rub. Actually speaking like a shrink is where the rubber meets the road. Right now you probably doubt that you can pull it off, and you are right. But there is an easy to follow program to get you up to speed. At the end of this chapter your confidence will soar so that you can hoodwink anyone that you are the healer you aspire to mimic.

Let's break it down in order:

Vocal Sounds
To Speak or Not To Speak
Word Choices
Acceptable Terms
Unacceptable Terms

Vocal Sounds

Before we talk about the actual choice of words, something needs to be said about how a therapist actually sounds. A good example is the way airline pilots speak over to the passengers in flight. Their voice is calming, soothing and confident. You just feel that everything is going to be all right even as you look out the window and notice you are in a pitched decline and realize things are clearly not all right. As the airplane jolts violently in the storm that these morons have inadvertently flown into, the pilot still speaks with assurance that "it's just a bit of rough air folks and everything will be ok." They have the voice of a therapist, helping you stay calm despite the flames.

It is important to remember, however, that a pilot is not a therapist, despite sounding like one. Pilots care about the machine they are operating, but there is no hard evidence that they actually care about you personally the way a therapist cares.

So now you must learn to sound like a soothing therapist. (For starters, lose your chicken cackle laugh. If your boisterous voice makes other people turn to look at you, ratchet back Scooter!) Imagine yourself in this situation: you come upon an accident where someone is injured. The non-therapist might yield to the impulse to cry out "Holy Crap!" This is clearly not therapeutic, as it further alarms the victim and discourages them from sharing. You, however, have the opportunity to react like a therapist by choosing to say something like, "I notice that you are bleeding from your ears. Is there a first aid kit in the wreckage?" Keep your volume low and your voice tone soothing, even breathy. This encourages dialogue and inspires trust. In may well lead to further opportunities such as riding in the ambulance with them and asking them how they feel?[9]

---

[9] In one such instance an individual behaved in just this way and found that they were later named in the person's will! Hey, you never know.

To Speak Or Not To Speak

The choice of speaking or not speaking is a decision that must be made on the fly and instantaneously. Mastering this choice and controlling that hair trigger impulse to just start jabbering is critical for the person who wants to be seen in a therapeutic light. The variables are few but critical. *They are:*

1. Silence
2. Clinical noises
3. Outright responding

Silence:
The most powerful weapon in the therapist's arsenal is dead silence. This is the secret to disarming the other person. In several speculative research observations in laboratory tests, silence by one person in a face-to-face encounter will inevitably elevate the the blood pressure of the other.[10] And this means they are stressed and now you're cooking! As their discomfort increases they are off their game, teetering with anxiety, this offers you the best opening to pierce through their weakened defenses. Now you are in charge of the encounter and can do with them what must be done: healing!

Clinical Noises:
The purpose of the clinical noise is to encourage, even prod the other to continue talking, even if incoherently. Remember: gathering information and data is power for a therapist (or you: the faux therapist).

There are 3 basic clinically approved noises to emit during an encounter:[11]

1. **"Hummm"** Expresses empathy & curiosity. Encourages more sharing and the illusion that you actually care about what they are saying

---

[10] As documented by a noticeable coloring of the face.
[11] Stick with these approved clinical noises. Avoid grunting or other guttural sounds as these will create clinical complications that will destroy the encounter.

2. **"Huh"** Expresses curiosity and urges more explanation without giving away your feeling that you think they are unstable

3. **"Mmmm"** Expresses sympathy for what has just been said, even if it has disgusted you

<u>Outright Responding:</u>

Here is an area where judgment and experience count. While maintaining a code of clinical silence in order to exercise power and solicit information through the approved clinical noises, there are surely times when your speaking is called for in the encounter. There are three triggers that should cause you to speak out loud:

1. **"Uncontrolled Weeping"** The person is no longer able to communicate. The sobbing can often be violent, so verbally reassuring them that you understand will prevent them from turning on you. *(Be careful and avoid the temptation to suggest "tissue?" as this stops their heaving and drives them backward)*

2. **"Periods of Prolonged Silence"** A common experience for a therapist when the client clams up for what seems like an eternity. Speaking is necessary to restart the conversation and preventing you from acting out impatiently and yelling at them. Berating them only reveals your own character weakness and puts a crimp in the trust. *Hello! Session over!* Even subtle indictors, such as making the 'move it along' finger swirl always backfires.

3. **"Physical Threat"** Trust your instincts here. Based on the history you have heard from the client, you can usually sense that the individual is prone to attack. Dealing with these types I always suggest sitting in a chair on rollers to facilitate retreat and having mace stored in the cushion by your dominant hand. In this instance raising you voice is appropriate whether commanding or begging mercy.

And finally concerning words you speak, remember this rule of thumb: *a therapist never changes the subject the client has chosen.* The client chooses the topic! Therapists stay right with them, realizing that there will be plenty of material available within that subject to steer and control the conversation.

Also, the therapist only admits to personal mistakes with their own clinical supervisor, never the client! Even if you realize you misspoke, *never yield!* This diminishes confidence in the therapist and is ultimately, if ironically a selfish act. Who are you thinking about here?[12]

<u>Word Choices</u>

When a therapist sees someone who appears to be very sad, of course they have the same thoughts as you do about them.[13] Observe what a shrink says to such a person. Yes, while they might be privately thinking, *"Wow this guy is a real Gloomy Gus!"* they don't speak that thought aloud. While you in such a situation might blurt out *"hey, lighten up man!"* the therapist calmly asks *"Are you doing okay?"* And, remembering from Chapter 1 above, it is spoken with the proper facial expression and physical distance.

What we learn from this is that the professional has learned to curtail their impulses, repressing the inclination to say what they actually think. That's the difference between them and you. But it is not as simple as choosing not to speak. The answer is not silence in the face of therapeutic opportunity. Again, just gaping silently at someone's suffering makes them think you are a heartless jackass, and would notice that people are inclined to walk away from you. But this rarely happens to a real therapist whose magnetism and charisma always invite people to remain, get closer, even stalk. It really comes down to what you say and how you say it. It comes down to word choices.

---

[12] The irony of this training is this: In the beginning it's not about you but the patient. But with healing it eventually does become all about you. I have dubbed this the Clinical Circle.
[13] Unless of course you are a sociopath in which case think about developing a parallel skill to fake it. Consider taking acting classes, e.g. Remember, there is more than one road to success!

As you practice the posture, facial expressions and vocal tone of a therapist, it is important that you not neglect what you say. It stands to reason that the words you use as a therapist are crucial to actually being effective. This means that even for you, who is not a real therapist, learning the right terms and phrases is, to say the least, important. *(A more detailed description of psychological terms is found later in the chapter)* For now let's focus on what to say in both casual and critical situations. The words you choose, your actual vocabulary plays a fundamental part in presenting a credible clinical appearance. Nothing is more jarring to a civilian than, having been persuaded by your therapeutic affect, you say things that shatter the illusion. Again this could result in an eruption of emotion and you might be attacked. You need to be prepared to defend yourself. And I don't mean with words, if you get my drift.[14]

The average person like you naturally selects words from your daily vocabulary. You may or may not have a large vocabulary at your disposal. For instance, whereas someone might say *"please pass the butter,"* you might blurt out, *"Yo! Gimme da butter."* Who will take you seriously as a therapist if you talk like a street urchin or hip hop teenager? But you see, it isn't about using big words, rather it's speaking in a more refined way.

Well what, you might ask, should I do if I'm like that other one, you know, the *"gimme"* person? Not to worry, you can overcome any limitation with a little practice and adding a few new terms to your limited, offensive vocabulary. It's not about a bias against your accent. Think about a real therapist who grew up in Brooklyn, New York or Birmingham, Alabama. Each will sound odd to others because of their thick accents. You might make a snap judgment that they sound stupid. But a little humility here, your accent probably makes them think you are a dumb ass too.[15] Listen to the words

---

[14] Dukes, T.R. *The Myth of the Passive Therapist: Clinical Retaliation Strategies (1946)*
[15] One former student, Mrs. Amy K, solved the issue by cultivating a refined British accent thus resolving the dilemma across all English speaking dialects. She reports always being mistaken for a therapist.

they are using. You can sound like a buffoon yet still come across as a therapist. The trick is in the words you choose.

Acceptable Terms

Let's come out of the gate fast here. There is an excellent term that can help you get started on learning to sound like a therapist right away. It's a complicated word invented by shrinks. It describes the approach used by mental health professionals when diagnosing others. But here's the beauty part: even just *using* the term, even if your comprehension of it is limited or foggy, will persuade people that you might really be a therapist. The are likely to step back in deference.

And what is this term?

The term is ... (wait for it) ...

BIOPSYCHOSOCIAL

Say it out loud - sound it out:

bio ...psycho ... social

Now put it together: **biopsychosocial!** Excellent. Say it aloud to a loved one several times until it sounds natural *(do not explain the term to them unless they are reading the book along with you).* Trust me, just peppering a casual conversation with this term puts civilians back on the defensive. And what's especially cool is that you can use the term in whole or even in parts!

Let's practice:
Once you have practiced saying the word out loud several times so your pronunciation is smooth, it's time to try it out in a sentence. Engage a family member or close friend in a casual conversation and bring up a well-publicized incident from the news where someone committed a crime. Start with an easy inquiry like *"wow, I wonder what's up with that guy?"* To which the other might say, *"yeah, he's nuts. Maybe he cracked his head in the tub?"* Here's your opening! You now casually say, *"Well, I'm certain he'll be evaluated with a battery of tests covering a biopsychosocial workup."* Often you'll find the person look at you curiously and mutter something like, *"oh yeah, I'm sure."* They won't want to reveal that they don't know what you know and feel stupid. And in this instance you will both know that they are correct. Who's like a therapist now?

This raises the critical issue of learning a whole new vocabulary. Surely you realize that therapists don't talk like other people. So it might be helpful to offer a brief glossary of acceptable and, importantly, unacceptable terms. Memorize the acceptable terms to use in your sentences (and make damn sure you avoid the unacceptable terms!).

Samples of Acceptable Therapeutic Terms *(with examples in a sentence)*:

Issues	*"Based on your outfit it seems you have self-esteem **issues**."*
Nature	*"So you're angry. No sense berating yourself for your dysfunctional **nature**."*
Nurture	*"We all feel the pain when we realize we have been damaged by our **nurture**."*
Cognitive	*"Sounds like with your confused thinking you might benefit from **cognitive** therapy."*
Unconscious	*"Hey, there's no shame. We all wrestle with our **unconscious** impulses."*
Conscious	*"Seems like she wasn't fully **conscious** of what she was saying or doing."*
Repression	*"Engaging a therapist can free you of a lot of those feelings locked in **repression**."*

Neurotic	*"Perhaps your father can't help himself and is struggling with his own **neurotic** conflicts."*
Inner child	*"Everyone conveys a strong outer presentation but often feels the sensitivity of our wounded **inner child**."*

<h2 style="text-align:center"><u>Unacceptable Terms</u></h2>

The words that a therapist should *never* utter are not really surprising and are usually quite intuitive. Any terms that directly convey judgment, anger, or aggression in any form are to be avoided like the bubonic plague. The exception of course is if you are directly quoting he client's own words. In this case, you can saying anything horrific and offensive *(as long as you make the quote signs with your fingers in the air)*.

<h3 style="text-align:center">Glossary of Unacceptable Therapeutic Terms</h3>
(try making up your own examples in a sentence):

The list is almost endless but commit to memorizing relevant negative terms and avoid them at all costs. You will certainly hear others use these terms. Your responsibility acting like a therapist is to substitute a preferred term.[16]

Here is a partial list of slurs and unacceptable terms you might encounter from your crude, non-therapist friends:

Crazy, Nuts, Crackers, Looney Tunes, Bonehead, Possessed, Loser, Numb Nuts, Idiot, Airhead, Birdbrain, Dimwit, Dolt, Demonic, Dork, Halfwit, knucklehead, Lamebrain, Lunkhead, Oaf, Pinhead, Witless, Cretin, Boob, Crackpot, Perfect Ass, Cuckoo, Daffy, Fool, Half-baked, Harebrained, Peabrain, Kooky, Lunatic, Nut Job, Sap, Screwball, Whack Job, Quack, Bats, Bonkers, Bughouse, Certifiable, Crackers, Crackpot, Demented, Deranged, Gaga, Haywire, Loco, Maniac, Screwy, Unhinged, Around the Bend, Off One's Gourd, Off One's Rocker, Out To Lunch,

---

[16] An exception is when sharing with other shrinks using the stress relief of gallows humor

Touched; Delusional, Paranoid, Oddball, Bananas, Berserk, Haywire, Hysterical Raving, Wigged Out

Also[17]:

In Britain: Gormless, Balmy, Cockeyed, Dotty

In Germany: Dunderhead

In Italy: Boombats

In Japan: クレイジー

In Russia: Sumashedshij

In Mexico: Loco

In China: 位疯狂的司机

In Sweden: Du är galen

---

[17] Whenever traveling abroad, be sure to memorize offensive terms in the local language

Chapter 3: On Being Like A Therapist: Heal Thyself

The foundation of therapeutic practice is understanding your own mental flaws and weaknesses. You've heard the proverb "physician, heal thyself." This refers to the temptation to believe that therapists are better than the other people they routinely encounter. While true, the therapist is always gracious and humble, acknowledging flaws inside themselves *(just not out loud or in any detail that can come back to bite us in the ass)*. But privately we must each evaluate our own psyches and figure put why we are in the state we are in emotionally. No easy task, but it is scut work that has to be done. No exceptions.

So how do we go about this terrifying task of exploring the self? Let's study using a map that can guide you along the path to deeper self-understanding and fulfillment. To follow this path you must:

1. **Assess Your Nature**
2. **Evaluate Your Nurture**
3. **Understand the Minefields of the Self**
4. **Embrace Supervision**

<u>Assessing Your Nature</u>

When it comes to behaving like a therapist, it all begins with the need to understand your own mental stability. What kind of shape are you in right now - psychologically speaking? Let's face it, if you are a train wreck, a dumpster fire or otherwise completely screwed up, it will add to the difficulty of pulling off this whole operation. This doesn't mean you can't do it. But you are in for a challenge that will cause hours of fear, trembling, and night sweats. It might have been logical, and even more merciful, to have discussed this at the beginning. However, it might have proven so demoralizing and crushing that you would have given up the entire enterprise before you got started. Then no one wins.

But shocking as this might be, don't give up, we're not done yet. In this chapter we will right your ship of state. I urge you to approach this chapter with openness and courage. Remember, each and everyone of you is psychologically complicated. Sure, some of you are more of a mess than others, but you all have issues. Let's look at the condition of your emotional landscape. Is the lawn of your psychological life green and healthy? Are there weeds here and there? Or is it burnt brown and riddled with emotional vermin? Face it, this is where we begin - the you of right now.

Let's start with some basics. Psychological health is based on two fundamental factors: your *nature* and your *nurture*. This means the basic biological equipment you were born with (nature) and the conditions of your home life growing up (nurture).

When it comes to your nature, that ship has sailed. You surely have some innate gifts, just likely not as many as others you see around you. Let's face it, If you're reading this and studying this program, your dreams are clearly reigned in. As far as your hopes for a great life of achievement, while there is surely still time, obviously you're no Bill Gates or Martha Stewart. Accept it. It isn't in your nature. And short of some surgical intervention, you have virtually no control over this part of you.

But what exactly is your personal nature? Can you describe it? One simple way to understand your nature is to think about which relative you most closely resemble. Take a moment and name the adult or adults in your life you are most like. Are you more like your biological mother or father? Are their parts of your grandparents, aunts, uncles or cousins who are like you? Ask your family to help you out. This is not just whom you most look like (some of those comparisons could rightfully horrify you) but whose personality most closely matches your own? (If the answer is 'no one' perhaps you were adopted in which case, you must work backwards and speculate what your biological ancestors were like.)

As you think about this, try to remain calm. If the answer is a relative who is an emotional disaster you are not doomed! Remember there are two factors, nature and nurture. Frequently one can help overcome the other. Most probably you are a fusion of several different ancestors who share the same traits. As you think about this composite, right a short paragraph describing your nature. It takes time to get the hang of it.

Here's the self-description of Lance in his first attempt at this exercise followed by his self description after a year of training:

> *" My nature? I don't know. I'm just Lance. That's it."*

And here is his second attempt after further training:

> *"Like my father, my uncle Ray and Aunt Sylvia, I am an extrovert of moderate intelligence. I tend to be impatient, probably have attention deficit disorder what I'm told is "limited range of emotion." This might be why I like to work with my fingers and not be bothered by a lot of crap from others."*

Now you try one for yourself. But remember, that's just half the picture of who you are!

SIDEBAR

What Are You?

Introvert or Extrovert

Even among non-professionals the terms Introvert and Extrovert are bandied around as if people knew what they were talking about. Clearly they don't (and frankly, neither do you). We often perceive them as people who are either "Shout Out" or "Shut Up" types. But just what do these terms mean technically? Here's some help:

EXTROVERT: From the Latin meaning *"outside"* (extra) and *"to turn"* (vertere). So an extrovert is someone who has *"turned outside"* themselves. They are exposing their innards, if you will. They are projecting their guts out to the rest of us, whether we want to receive it or not. It's like having their personality involuntarily projectile vomited onto another. These are people who just won't shut the hell up. Sometimes they are charming but just as often they are loud and annoying. In many cases their constant yapping means they are usually rude, impulsive and therefore untrustworthy because they typically speak before they think.

INTROVERT: From the Latin meaning *"inward"* (intro) and *"to turn"* (vertere). So an Introvert is someone who has *"turned inside"* on themselves. Their thoughts and feelings are wrapped up inside them like mummies and do not get expressed. They are entombed inside themselves tighter than King Tut. While this can be pleasant for those around them because they don't talk much, the price they pay is significant. For one thing, they often repress their feelings that churn inside them like a mixer and eat away at their stomach lining. Before long their guts look like mashed potatoes and they are always running to the can for their irritable bowel syndrome. And in addition, you never really know what they are thinking and consequently have good reason to be suspicious of them.

As you practice your therapeutic behavior be on the alert for each of these types. You've been warned!

Assessing Your Nurture

Even if your upbringing was terrible, it nonetheless has given you many assets. Let's face it, here you are reading a book on how to appear to be a therapist. That says something![18] The point here is that how your family treated you growing up determined a lot of what you have now become. Perhaps there was chaos, conflict and conniptions. Maybe it was wealth, privilege and peace. Either way, when you combine your nature with this nurture - *VOILA!* - out pops the you of now! So let's get busy with the task of reshaping this mess of you into the therapeutic juggernaut you long to become. We are closing in on the finished project.

These two sections, nature and nurture, are brief because there is really not a lot to be said. You are already either adjusted, screwed or probably somewhere in the middle. What we can do is move forward. But first a short word on a phenomenon that ties the nature and nurture situation together: It's called "Your Inner Child."

Your Inner Child

This concept is helpful for people to understand how their early life remains alive within them. This inner child is like a being within, like in the movie *Alien*, that overrides and directs your thoughts and feelings. This inner child is usually vulnerable and innocent, but can also be petulant and bratty. Think of the typical two year old. They are helpless and needy. They cannot feed themselves or manage their personal hygiene. They have severe mood swings from sweet, delightful joy to murderous fury and rage in an instant.[19]

Now imagine this complicated little two year old as being still alive and active right inside you - OMG! On the outside you look *like* the adult parent.

---

[18] Although perhaps this is being read to you. Maybe you are vision impaired, in which case I am sorry. Or maybe you have other significant limitations. Again sorry.

[19] It does seem disturbing to describe a little child in such harsh terms. But this is what Sigmund Freud discovered - children can be little containers of rage. Their tiny appearance masks this reality and they are impotent to act on it since they just don't have the weaponry.

But inside is this creature that can push its way out into the open at the drop of a hat. One minute others see you as a "cutie pie", the next an unhinged, snarling reptile! This inner child must be alternately loved and disciplined. You are both the parent and the child in one. (Isn't it obvious why real therapists have to go the school for, like, *forever!?*)

Minefields of the Self
The Defense Mechanisms

Now we come to the dangers lurking within your personality that I call the "Minefields of the Self." The technical name is "Defense Mechanisms" because we use them as mechanisms for our defense - no small matter. A defense mechanism is a strategy used as protection from psychological stress. We learn these strategies as children in response to horrendous things that happen to us. While they seem to work, defense mechanisms are the very behaviors that completely screw up your life. They do this by preventing you from facing any reality that might otherwise crush your spirits like a ant on the hot cement. The average person sees someone using a defense mechanism and instantly dismisses the person as a head case. While true, this term is unprofessional.[20] The job of a therapist is to slowly expose defensive behaviors so you can stop using them.

There are loads of defense mechanisms available to us. Let's review a sample of the most obvious that you, posing as a therapist, can possibly identify. And here's the cool advantage you have. Since most defense mechanisms are unconscious to the person using them, you get to see them before they do! This is real power!

---

[20] In fact, why not go back to the unacceptable terms section and pencil in the term 'head case' as an addition.

Here are the most common of the almost limitless defenses mechanisms that human beings employ (which ones are you using right now?)

Denial: This is pretty obvious to anyone who has watched *Oprah* or *Jerry Springer*. It refers to the defense of pretending something is not happening even as it is apparent to everyone else. It's like when your uncle insists he doesn't have a drinking problem yet he has obviously spit up on his shirt and his car is all dented and has busted headlights. *Denial*

Regression: This is a really cool one because it is usually so bizarre. It's when someone reverts to a behavior they used when they were very young. When you confront your boss that there is growing dissatisfaction among the workers, he begins to suck his thumb even as he continues to speak. *Regression*

Acting Out: The term itself describes the defense. Instead of reacting rationally when feeling threatened, the individual immediately acts out their emotion. In some instances, like when someone is physically threatened, acting out is appropriate. But not so when your brother hurls his cocktail glass at the TV screen when Dr. Phil mentions the term *"gender dysphoria."* *Acting Out*

Dissociation: A really spooky defense where an individual suddenly takes on a completely different persona (i.e., personage) with little apparent warning. When uncomfortable at a family reunion, for instance, your cousin Lou comes to the dinner table wearing a football uniform complete with that black stuff under his eyes. *Dissociation*

Projection: A form of the circular "I know you are, but what am I" argument among children, when unable to face their own tendencies, the person accuses the other of having the same problem they have. It would be like the Pope screaming at a Cardinal: "You are so damn high and mighty! You think your better than the rest of us!" *Projection*

Repression: Stuffing uncomfortable feelings so deep in your unconscious that the only indication that you are doing so are the physical symptoms that erupt. At an annual holiday dinner with visiting family you have diarrhea for a week and yet don't make the connection between this and your disgust for them. *Repression*

Reaction Formation: A real head spinner, this defense is when you turn one emotional feeling into its opposite behavior! Like when you Aunt Phyllis talks openly about her admiration for her mother when you know for a fact that she would actually like to throw a plate of food at her head. *Reaction Formation*

Compartmentalization: Like the word itself, this is where you put two competing behaviors into different mental boxes. Like your friend who devotes hours to volunteering at a charity for the homeless poor but who is simultaneously pilfering cash and supplies supplies from their office, unaware of what a duplicitous ass he is being. *Compartmentalization*

A Practice Self Diagnosis
(Start by using yourself as the patient)

ARE YOU STRESSED OUT?

Are there times when you wonder if the pressure might be getting to you? Do you find some things funny when others do not? Or, do you feel sad when those around you are laughing? Perhaps you have come to a place in your life where you are questioning your own stability. It could be that you are experiencing high levels of stress. By taking the following quiz, you will not only discover what might be wrong with you; it will heal you at the same time. Isn't that great?

SYMPTOMS
(Answer YES or NO)

1. When I enter a room full of family or friends, conversation stops. **Y/N**
2. I sometimes become hyper-focused on a small object (e.g., an insect or the pattern on someone's tie) and lose track of what I had been doing. **Y/N**
3. Routine errands to the store cause me to fear for my life. **Y/N**
4. While watching television, I sometimes talk back to the screen. **Y/N**
5. In order to remain calm, I often have to breathe into a paper bag. **Y/N**
6. Bathing has become exhausting. **Y/N**
7. When sitting alone in a room, I find myself staring blankly with my mouth hanging wide open. **Y/N**
8. Without any prior experience or preparation, I have begun a dangerous new hobby (bungee jumping, e.g.). **Y/N**
9. At least once each week, I spend one hour hiding under a piece of furniture in my home. **Y/N**
10. In spite of my awareness about the negative consequences, I am consistently, physically attracted to individuals with whom I have little or nothing in common. **Y/N**

DIAGNOSIS
How many "yes" answers did you have?

0-3 _You are in excellent shape_ There are very few indications of serious stress in your life. If, in spite of this low score, you still feel that you are seriously stressed, the problem may be unconscious. Speaking with a trained psychotherapist about your past life experiences may help you unlock the key to your distorted sense of reality.

4-6 _You are experiencing moderate stress_ Obviously enough symptoms are present to warrant your attention. Try a new regimen of physical and deep breathing exercises, and consider seeking the help of a trained mental health professional about strategies for relaxing, recouping energy, and regaining perspective.

7-10 _You are under significant stress_ Your health is at risk. But remain calm; you will probably be fine. But it is imperative that you regain your composure and reconnect with other people to regroup and reassert your boundaries. You should schedule an appointment with your physician and also a trained mental health professional. There are excellent treatments available and you can feel better in before you know it. And even if you wind up being institutionalized, I'm still betting on you!

Chapter 4: Understanding Symptoms & Treatment

Symptoms

This is where the rubber meets the road. Let's face it, if a real therapist cannot identify symptoms, they're screwed, plain and simple. A shrink who cannot identify a symptom is like a trucker who can't drive a standard transmission, an accountant with severe dyslexia, a visually impaired baseball pitcher, an actor who stutters. The job just can't be done. So if you intend to behave like a competent therapist you need to become literate about symptoms.

What is a symptom? It comes from a Greek word *"symptoma"* that means essentially, you know, a *symptom*. It's a sign or indication of something going on. For instance if someone starts sweating whenever you mention your pet snake, the sweating is a symptom of their anxiety about snakes, their fear of snakes.[21]

Sigmund Freud was a famous physician who invented the treatment he called psychoanalysis. This is a technique used by many therapists designed to uncover problems you have that are buried in your unconscious. You have repressed them and they are rumbling around in your psyche like a caged rat. They are the feelings and memories of past experiences that you are trying to forget, but your body just will not cooperate. You only know that these repressed feelings are there because of the weird symptoms telling us something is afoot inside. If, for example, an individual begins to blink rapidly *(symptom)* when they see a hot dog vendor, it raises the curiosity of the therapist that there is some connection to be explored. Perhaps they are the child of a disappointed hot-dog vendor parent. Maybe they were assaulted by a frankfurter as a young child. These repressed memories would reveal themselves in the physical symptom as they smell sauerkraut or even seeing a jar of mustard. You see how complicated this all is and how unlikely you will ever fully master this area? So where do you turn for help?

---

[21] This symptom is a sign for you to shut your yapper about your freaking snake, Einstein!

As mentioned earlier, real therapists use the *Diagnostic And Statistical Manual of Mental Disorders*, simply referred to as the *DSM V*.[22] I remind you to conspicuously carry the book around, and even carefully refer to it in conversations, such as "Gee, Pete, I need to see what the DSM says about that?" Inside you will notice that this complex book documents every conceivable category of mental health and illness known to humanity, including your own.[23] But be careful. If you misuse this resource your could do harm to others by pretending you understand it. So it behooves you to generally avoid going to deep into this resource or you run the risk of getting calls from attorneys and spam from online universities.

To help you understand the complex world of psychological symptoms here are some illustrations. Since you are unlikely to quickly master the actual list of symptoms in the DSM, there are some shortcuts to help you. Let's take a look at some alternative ways to diagnose common conditions.

---

[22] Don't say "DSM 5." Just say "the DSM" so a real therapist doesn't think your a piker.
[23] For fun, look up 'narcissism' and 'grandiosity.' You'll get a chuckle!

Symptom Scenario 1

You are riding in a car with your girl friend and you hear that she is quietly humming a song. You listen carefully and identify the tune as the Joan Jett hit, "I Hate Myself for Loving You."

What do you suspect?
a) She identifies with Joan Jett's appearance?
b) She is unconsciously revealing her anger with you for reasons you can perhaps identify?
c) The reference is to another individual in her life whom you can identify?

What do you do?
a) Hum along and see if she takes a hint and talks about her feelings
b) Calmly start a conversation about how hard human relationships are to endure
c) Angrily confront her and ask bluntly, "are you referring to me!?"

Symptom Scenario 2

During a staff meeting the boss raises the subject of petty cash pilferage in a joking manner. Everyone laughs but suddenly a colleague has a sudden coughing fit, gets up and leaves the room.

What do you suspect?
a) The individual might be guilty of theft
b) It triggered a reaction to an earlier life incident where their own petty cash was stolen by a trusted ally
c) They have a condition

What do you do
a) Launch a discreet investigation into the matter and offer to mediate with the authorities as a their counselor
b) Rat out the person to the boss and authorities
c) Give them your card and tell them "I'm here for you."

Symptom Scenario 3

Chatting with a friend who is an airline pilot she shares that her newly assigned co-pilot is "odd." When you ask for specifics she relates how the pilot often seems to have a cold and is sniffing constantly which has become a real distraction. In addition he speaks so rapidly it's hard to understand him and he is constantly talking during landing. When confronted politely about being a bit quieter he flew into a rage and threw a water bottle at the instrument panel.

What do you suspect?
a) The pilot is an upbeat personality who has a chronic sinus condition
b) The pilot may have a substance abuse problem, specifically cocaine addiction
c) Your friend is too serious and needs to chill

What do you do?
a) Report the pilot to your supervisor.
b) Discreetly ask for a transfer to another crew
c) Wear a wire and send Incriminating information to the news media

Symptom Scenario 4

You're father has been really quiet for several weeks, often spending full days in his room staring at the wall. When you ask if there is anything wrong, he just mutters, "nothing." You suspect he is depressed until one day a truck delivers several boxes of electronic equipment to the house in his name. You also notice that there is a new luxury car in the driveway. When you ask him about it, he is now suddenly dressed in loud clothing and gleefully opening his boxes.

What do you suspect?
a) He has come out of his depression!
b) He is having a manic episode and is bipolar
c) He's gone insane

What do you do?
a) Joyfully celebrate his new happy state of mind
b) Calmly confront him with his need for treatment
c) Ignore him since his problems have obviously gone away

Symptom Scenario 5

Your cousin is having a severe grief reaction at the loss of his pet ferret and emotionally withdraws. You find out that he has left his home and disappeared. After an investigation you accompany his family to retrieve him from a small town in Canada where he has been seen. When confronted he denies his identity, asserts his new name and position with a local exterminator. Against his will his family has him committed for treatment

What do you suspect?
a) He has had a head injury
b) Despite their certainty this is not in fact their family member
c) He has suffered a rare form of amnesia and is in a fugue state

What do you do?
a) Since he seems happy let him live out his life where he is living
b) Ask him if you can have his old stuff
c) If he had a better lifestyle than your own, take his place and everyone wins

Treatment

Actually treating someone as a therapist is what is known in the trade as "boots on the ground." Honestly if you can identify symptoms but don't know know what to do next, you are clinically useless. In fact, this is where you are right now and will remain. And importantly, this is as far as this train can go with you on board. We've stopped at the "Fauxtown" station and this is where you disembark as the real therapists ride on. They move forward to engage the patient and turn their known symptoms back around on them. It's like shrink jujitsu. So where does this leave you? Stranded in "No-where-ville?" Calm down, there is a bit more to learn.

As someone learning to behave like a therapist you can master your observational skills about the world of treatment options that your real counterparts employ. While you are not allowed to sit in on real clinical sessions there are options. The first one is *meh*, but the other two are way cool options:

1. You do have the option of making the painful choice and financial sacrifice of going through formal education right through graduate school. But seriously, with what you have learned here in this quick read, what's the upside to this option? Merely behaving like a shrink gives you most of the real benefits of the profession yet saves thousands of dollars and unimaginable time dealing with professors and administrators. It also avoids the sticky wicket of sitting for hours listening to goofball clients and the nightmare of wrestling with insurance companies.

2. A better option is to shadow a real therapist. Now it will be important to tell them what you are doing.[24] But here's the skinny. Ask around for the name of a therapist in your town. Meet with them and tell them you are considering going into the field and wonder if they would befriend you.

---

[24] I do NOT recommend that you share this book with them. This might well be professionally offensive to them as you are having their secrets revealed for the cost of a cheap book.

Tell them you will eventually like to become a client (stressing that you will be a full fee patient without needing insurance claims). Arrange an hour a week to accompany them to a coffee shop, a local luncheonette or a community meeting. Your purpose is to watch how they interact. But NOT WITH YOU! How are they interacting with others, strangers or casual acquaintances they encounter. This is the gold standard for acting like a therapist, because you are watching and mimicking a real therapist behaving like a real therapist. *Capiche?*

3. The third and best option is even more potent. Given what you have learned about your own nature and nurture in Chapter 3, it's obvious you can easily become a patient yourself. This is an amazing learning opportunity where you can watch and feel how your own therapist will take your symptoms (many of which you are not aware you exhibit) and flip them over on you to make a treatment plan designed to actually cure you! How about them apples? Suddenly you witness first hand how your simple, insipid stories can result in you being on medication and in weekly sessions, shivering and weeping like a child! It's a fantastic opportunity that you should seriously consider. It's like going to treatment school!

No matter which option you pick, remember that you are close to becoming an actual faux therapist. **Absorb the learning and for the love of God, DO NOT ATTEMPT TO TREAT ANYONE!** You're playing with fire my friend and you can get burned.[25] With this a caution in mind, get out there and become the visage of the therapist you know you can imagine yourself to be!

But before we end this, let's look at some case studies that will help you get a picture of therapy in real time. Let's help hone your craft!

---

[25] If I learn that you have ignored this warning and wind up in the judicial system I will fully and aggressively retaliate with my legal team to protect the integrity of the system you have learned and abused. My lawyers will burn you down, boyo!

Chapter 5: Honing Your Craft: Clinical Case Studies

Stories From The Couch

The following are real case studies taken from Dr. Will's files and made available for purposes of training you to be like a real therapist. You are not allowed to share these stories with anyone outside of the course. In addition, you are strictly for bidden to engage in any attempts to learn the real identities of these individuals. Failure to comply will result in immediate expulsion from the course and confiscation of all materials.

CASE STUDY 1[26]

The Sober Teen Who Claimed He Was An Addict

Presenting Problem: Steven, a 17 year-old High School junior is home schooled by his single mother and her two unmarried, twin sisters. With the lone exception of an inadvertent shoplifting incident when he was 4, he's never been in trouble. One day he announced to his mother that he'd been attending meetings of Narcotics Anonymous for a year. When asked about his drug use he replied, "no, I'm sober now, thanks to the program." His mother pressed if he had used drugs before. "No, but I realized I was an addict and wanted to 'nip it in the bud'." His two Aunts grilled him for several hours but he clung to his story. "You just don't understand! You're all clueless. Only my program mates get it. Thank God for my N.A. family." Eventually Stephen was given up for adoption.

Your Diagnosis: Describe Steven's issue in your own words.

Steven is:
a) Delusional and in need of medication for a psychotic episode
b) Trapped in a smothering maternal world

Your Treatment: What would you suggest for a treatment plan?

Steven Needs:
a) A visit to a detoxification ward to look at real addicts
b) Steven is not the real patient, the lunatic adults need the intervention
c) Corporal Punishment
d) Seek an alternative living and schooling arrangement in another state

Correct Answers: (shown in reverse: hold a mirror up to the page for the correct answers) b d

---

[26] Use the bottom of the page to make notes. You must submit them with your final exam. No exceptions!

CASE STUDY 2

The Senior Citizen Who Burned Down His Facility

Presenting Problem: Douglas is an 87 year old retired produce manager who lives in Fargo Senior Village, a retirement facility in North Dakota. Douglas was a decorated combat veteran in WWII whose unit invaded a German stronghold where he used a flamethrower to save his squad. He was placed in his current facility by his five grown children, all of whom live in San Diego, California *(this is where Douglas also lived his entire life)*. The reason for the move so far from home was years of conflict with his children and their families. They have accused him of setting fire to each of their homes over the course of several decades. In each instance he would wait for the fire department's arrival and take photos of the action and use them for his Christmas card. He came for court ordered treatment when arrested for setting fire to Fargo Senior Village.

Your Diagnosis: Describe Douglas' issue in your own words.

Douglas is:
a) A sociopath arsonist
b) Delusional senior suffering Post Traumatic Stress Disorder with onset of dementia.

Your Treatment: What would you suggest for a treatment plan?

Douglas Needs:
a) Relocation to a Veteran's Facility with military honors
b) The death penalty
c) Incarceration in a minimum security facility
d) Inpatient treatment for his impulse disorder of pyromania

Correct Answers: (shown in reverse: hold a mirror up to the page for the correct answers) b d

CASE STUDY 3

The Flamboyant Postal Worker

<u>Presenting Problem</u>: Lois is a 41-year-old postal carrier in a large city serving the exact same route for 18 years. She is highly popular with the community due to her habit of dressing up for work in a variety of costumes while delivering the mail. Over the years she has shown up as a Police Swat Team member, a clown in full makeup, and recently the Dowager from *Downton Abbey*. While amusing many over the years, her supervisors who were generally tolerant of her odd behavior have sent her to counseling after a recent incident. Lois came dressed as Wonder Woman when the small dog of a teenager along her route growled at her. She used a lasso to detain the boy and demanded to know what the dog was saying about her.

<u>Your Diagnosis</u>: Describe Lois' issue in your own words.

<u>Lois</u>:
a) Has Dissociative Identity Disorder (Multiple Personality)
b) Psychosis with Exhibitionist features

<u>Your Treatment</u>: What would you suggest for a treatment plan?

<u>Lois Needs</u>:
a) Medication and weekly psychotherapy
b) Institutionalization
c) Service award for promoting community morale
d) A week's suspension with pay

Correct Answers: (shown in reverse: hold a mirror up to the page for the correct answers) ꓐ ꓐ

CASE STUDY 4

The School Bus Driver Who Lost It

Presenting Problem: Bridget is a 72-year-old retiree who works part time as a bus driver for a Consolidated School District in Texas. She served in the Navy for 35 years as a cook and still wears her uniform every day. She treats the elementary school children riding with her like a military unit, often yelling and issuing orders. She does an inspection of their clothing and decorum before she starts the route. She has been disciplined by the district and narrowly evaded lawsuits from angry parents. It culminated one afternoon on a typical Wednesday run when a seven year old began to vomit in the aisle. She ordered all the children to clean the mess using buckets of soapy water she always kept on the bus. She was suspended and ordered to go to counseling.

Your Diagnosis: Describe Bridget's issue in your own words.

Bridget:
a) Suffers from an Adjustment Disorder
b) Obsessive Compulsive Disorder

Your Treatment: What would you suggest for a treatment plan?

Bridget Needs:
a) Anger Management Classes
b) Deprogramming by the U.S. Navy
c) Medication for her Obsession
d) None of the Above

Correct Answers: (shown in reverse: hold a mirror up to the page for the correct answers) ɔ ɐ

CASE STUDY 5

The Dad Who Thought He Was Maury Povich

Presenting Problem: Curtis is a 41 year old railroad engineer. He and his wife have six daughters ranging in age from 11 through 22 years old. He became suspicious when he realized that none of his daughters bore any physical resemblance to him or relatives on his side of the family. Their facial shapes, hair color, skin tone, height and body shape were each unique. He told his wife who chuckled and left the room. That's when Curtis began his obsession with genetic testing. He researched and taught himself all he could learn about genetics and began taking DNA samples of his family, discreetly collecting hair samples and including his own mouth swab to send to a Mexican laboratory. He asked for comparisons. When the results came back he planned to announce the findings at an extended family reunion. To his surprise and dismay all the girls were confirmed as his own. But it also found that he himself was the son of the only couple executed for treason during the Vietnam War and was put up for adoption.

Your Diagnosis: Describe Curtis' issue in your own words.

Curtis:
a) Has Paranoid Personality Disorder
b) Adjustment Disorder

Your Treatment: What would you suggest for a treatment plan?

Curtis Needs:
a) Medication and weekly psychotherapy
b) Treatment for Post Traumatic Stress Disorder
c) A retreat sponsored by Ancestry.com
d) All of the Above

Correct Answers: (shown in reverse: hold a mirror up to the page for the correct answers) 6 6

CASE STUDY 6

The Minister Who Botched His Message

Presenting Problem: Reverend Bob is a Presbyterian Minister serving an elderly congregation in a suburban Cleveland community. He has been the pastor for 21 years and was ordered to come to counseling by his Board after an incident one Sunday during the service. Known for his easy and gentle demeanor he shocked the congregation when he stopped suddenly in the middle of his message on kindness and bellowed, "can't someone shut that kid up? I swear to Zeus that if I hear one more peep I'll come down there and put the sock of his father in his little yapper! Now let's continue ..." But the damage was done and realizing what he had just done he covered his face and ran from the church and boarded a bus for New Orleans. He was found by his family a year later working for a landscaper and returned home. He comes for treatment with no memory of the events.

Your Diagnosis: Describe Eddie's issue in your own words.

Eddie:
a) Suffers from Intermittent Explosive Disorder
b) A Fugue Amnesia State

Your Treatment: What would you suggest for a treatment plan?

Eddie Needs:
a) Past Life Regression Therapy
b) Treatment for Depression
c) Anger Management Classes
d) All of the Above

Correct Answers: (shown in reverse: hold a mirror up to the page for the correct answers) b d

Final Exam

(You are almost home!)

Answer these ten True or False questions as our final exam.

IMPORTANT: This is *NOT* an open book exam. Do not refer back in the text!

Question 1: A therapist always uses a very expressive face.

Question 2: A therapist always speaks in a loud voice

Question 3: A therapist believes that one's nature condemns them

Question 4: A therapist believes that one's nurture condemns them

Question 5: A therapist believes the inner child is a sick myth

Question 6: A therapist believes that repression is healthy

Question 7: A therapist believes swearing at a client is helpful

Question 8: A therapist always remains quiet when being physically attacked

Question 9: A therapist usually uses rapid eye blinking as an approach

Question 10: A therapist can use grunting as a strategy for sharing

BONUS QUESTION: (worth the weight of 4 questions above)

Gumby is made of: a) wood b) putty c) metal

(mail your answers to the psychology department of a nearby University)

OATH

I *(state your name)* **of** *(state your home town and state)* **swear to use my newly acquired skill to appear and behave like a real therapist only for good and ethical profit. I will refrain from diagnosing others out loud and will resist engaging in any behavior that can be construed as therapeutic treatment.**

So help me *(state your higher power)*

CERTIFICATE OF COMPLETION

Add your own name & artwork

Made in the USA
San Bernardino, CA
24 July 2014